Young Thomas Edison

MICHAEL DOOLING

Holiday House
New York

For Jane, as always

The author would like to thank Steve Williams,
T. J. Gaffney, and Gloria Justice, of the Port Huron Museum,
for their help.

Copyright © 2005 by Michael Dooling
All Rights Reserved
Printed in the United States of America
The text typeface is Goudy Catalog.
The illustrations for this book were painted
in oil paint on linen canvas.
www.holidayhouse.com
First Edition
1 3 5 7 9 10 8 6 4 2

Library of Congress Cataloging-in-Publication Data
Dooling, Michael.
Young Thomas Edison / by Michael Dooling.— 1st ed.
p. cm.
Includes bibliographical references.
ISBN 0-8234-1868-5
1. Edison, Thomas A. (Thomas Alva), 1847–1931—Juvenile literature.
2. Edison, Thomas A. (Thomas Alva), 1847–1931—
Childhood and youth—Juvenile literature.
3. Inventors—United States—Biography—Juvenile literature.
4. Electric engineers—United States—
Biography—Juvenile literature. I. Title.

TK140.E3D77 2004
621.3'092—dc22
2004049345

ISBN-13: 978-0-8234-1868-8
ISBN-10: 0-8234-1868-5

THOMAS ALVA EDISON was born in a little house in Milan, Ohio, on February 11, 1847, to Samuel and Nancy Edison. He was the youngest of seven children.

Thomas, who was called Young Al by his family, lived in an era very different from ours. There was no electric light, no telephone, no radio or CD player, not even a movie theater.

Thomas loved to experiment. In 1856, at the age of nine, he turned his family's cellar into a laboratory complete with test tubes, beakers, and whatever chemicals he could buy. It was a mess—bottles were everywhere. Young Al would mix one chemical after another, sometimes following the experiments in his chemistry book—sometimes not. "A little of this and a little of that," he used to mumble.

His mother always encouraged him to ask questions, and he did. What is this? Why does that happen? How does it happen?

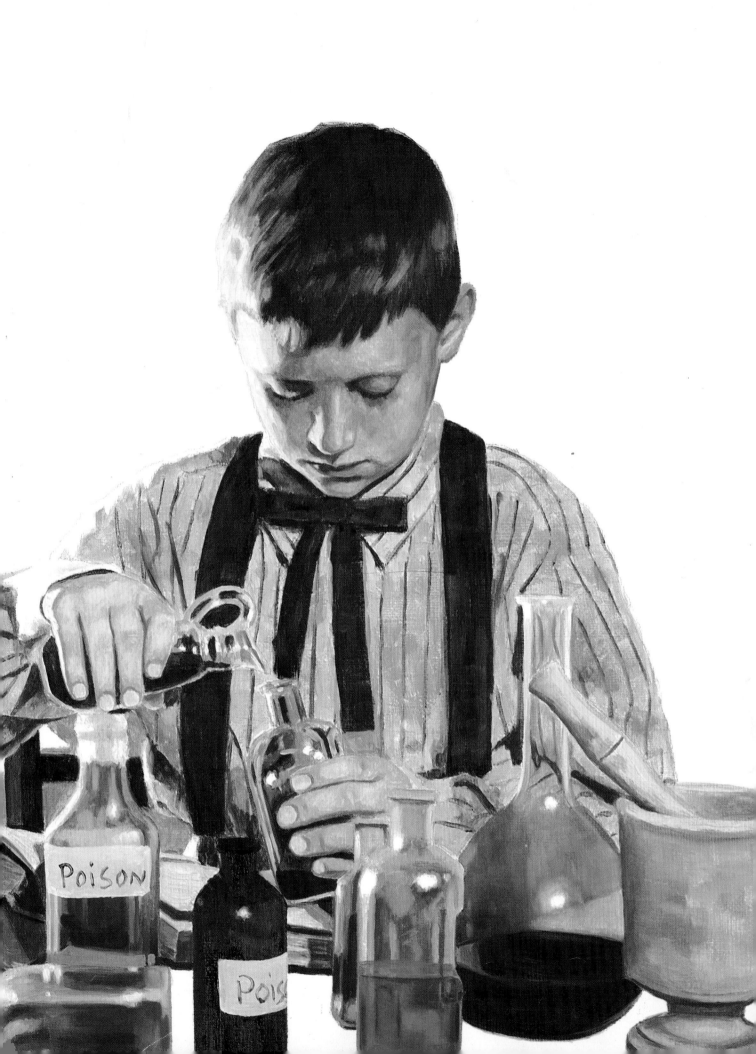

A bout of scarlet fever left Al hard of hearing, which made school difficult. While Al asked many questions at home, he did not ask any at school. Instead he spent his time there daydreaming about his next experiment.

Al was always in trouble. One day his teacher called him addled and made him sit in the corner. Al's mother was so upset by this that she took him out of school after only three months. She knew that Al was not addled—he was a genius. School was too slow for him.

From then on Al's mother, a former teacher, taught him at home. Mrs. Edison made sure he received an excellent education. He read Shakespeare, the Bible, history, and much more. Over the next few years he also studied the great inventors, such as Galileo.

At age twelve Young Al decided to look for a job. He needed money to continue his experiments. So he went into business as a paperboy on the train that went from Port Huron, where the Edisons now lived, to Detroit, Michigan. Every morning from 7 A.M. to 10 A.M. Al sold newspapers.

Then he spent all day at the Detroit library, reading and dreaming about his next experiment. He planned to read every book in the library, starting with the last book on the shelf and working back to the first. At night he took the train home and sold papers again.

Eventually, with the permission of the conductor, Al set up a laboratory in the baggage car of the train. Soon the young scientist was experimenting with everything: chemicals, gadgets, test tubes, beakers, doohickeys, and thingamajigs.

Every morning Al continued to sell newspapers on the Grand Trunk Railway. Always ambitious, he expanded his line of goods to include fruits and candies. By day he would study at the library or do experiments in the baggage car, which he had completely taken over.

Al usually carried a book in his pocket and was always thinking about his next experiment. His days were exhausting—but he loved every second.

After the Civil War began, everyone wanted the latest news. One day Al sold a thousand newspapers! With such a demand, Al decided to start his own newspaper. He bought a secondhand press and set up shop in the baggage car, next to his laboratory. *The Weekly Herald* sold for eight cents per month and soon reached a circulation of four hundred copies. Fifteen-year-old Al Edison was on top of the world—newsboy, salesman, businessman, and scientist.

Things were going well until one day when the train made a sudden lurch. Bottles, books, newspapers, candies, and fruits went flying—along with Al. A bottle of phosphorus burst into flames. Al scrambled to put out the flames, but they spread too fast. Soon a very upset conductor rushed in. He was so mad that he boxed Al's ears. This worsened Al's hearing problem. At the next stop the conductor threw all of Al's things off the train—even him!

Al had never been so disappointed in his life. He went home and set up his laboratory again with the encouragement of his mother. He continued to experiment and tinker with every gadget he could get his hands on. Usually his experiments did not work—but he always kept trying.

Before long Al had another job. He was a "night wire"—a railroad telegraph operator—in Stratford Junction, Canada. There was a lot to learn. For weeks, he soaked up all the information he could about telegraphy.

Al learned Morse code and much more. He worked the 7 P.M. to 7 A.M. shift, often sleeping right in the station. He also set up his laboratory in the back room of the station so that he could experiment in his off-hours. Apart from the occasional explosion life was grand.

One of Al's duties as the operator was to send the signal 6 every hour on the hour to show the dispatcher at the next station that he was awake. But the long hours sometimes caught up with him and he would fall asleep, so the scientist in him had an idea. Soon Al had invented a device that hooked the telegraph key to a clock. When the hour struck, the minute hand of the clock sent the message 6 for him. It was a moment of pure genius, which quickly got him fired when his boss discovered he was sleeping on the job.

For the next five years, young Edison traveled all over the South and Midwest from one telegraph job to another. He continued to try to find ways to improve the telegraph. At age twenty-one he made his way to Boston, Massachusetts, and started using his first name, Thomas. He decided that he was going to be an inventor, and he set up his latest laboratory. He wanted to learn all he could about electrical forces. His first patented invention was the *Electrical Vote Recorder*. Unfortunately, Congress did not like his invention and he could not sell it.

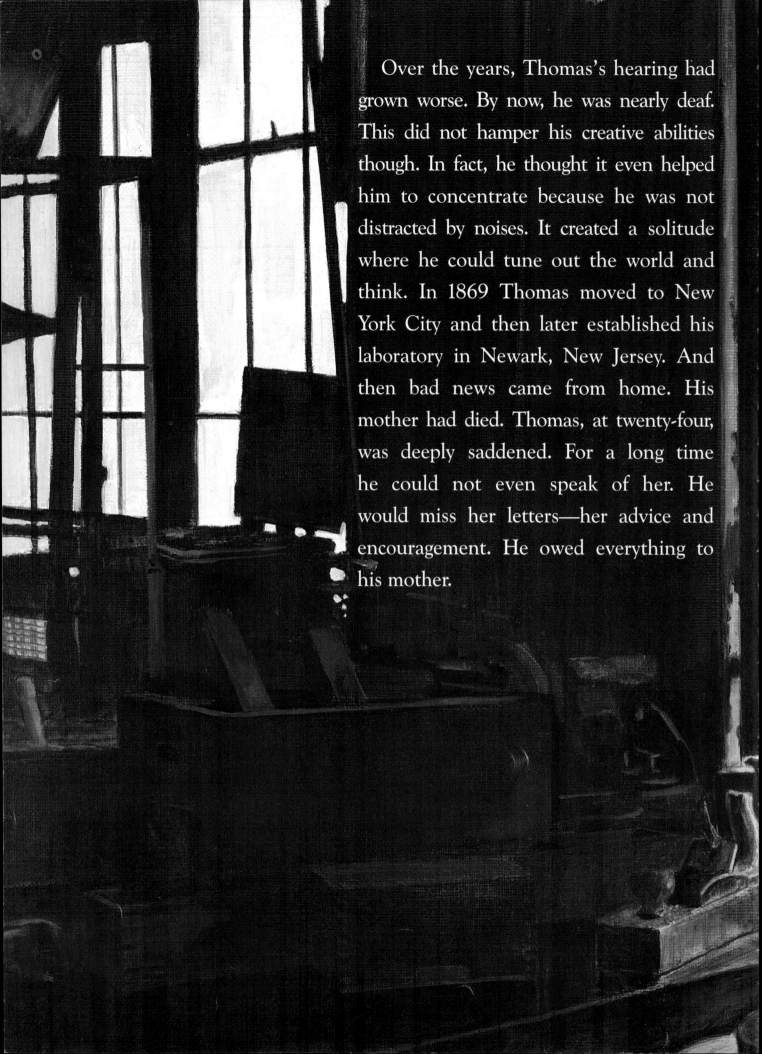

Over the years, Thomas's hearing had grown worse. By now, he was nearly deaf. This did not hamper his creative abilities though. In fact, he thought it even helped him to concentrate because he was not distracted by noises. It created a solitude where he could tune out the world and think. In 1869 Thomas moved to New York City and then later established his laboratory in Newark, New Jersey. And then bad news came from home. His mother had died. Thomas, at twenty-four, was deeply saddened. For a long time he could not even speak of her. He would miss her letters—her advice and encouragement. He owed everything to his mother.

In 1876 Thomas moved his laboratory to Menlo Park, New Jersey. He invented the *carbon transmitter,* which amplified the human voice—making the telephone and microphone possible. He also invented a machine that talked—a *phonograph.* Shortly thereafter, Thomas invented an *electric lightbulb.* He also discovered the principle of sound waves, which made the radio possible. In 1887 he moved his laboratory to West Orange, New Jersey, developing the *motion picture* and much more. At one point he had 250 people working for him and 45 inventions going.

Such strange, incredible inventions were coming out of his laboratory that people started to call Thomas "The Wizard." He would live to be eighty-four years old and patent 1,093 inventions. Thomas would always remember his mother's encouraging words to ask questions. What is this? Why does that happen? How does it happen?

1877 Tinfoil Phonograph

The first recording of sound. Sound was recorded on tinfoil wrapped around the cylinder. A message was shouted into the cone (which was attached to the cylinder) as the cylinder was cranked by hand. Sound was reproduced by cranking the cylinder again. The first recorded words were "Mary had a little lamb."

1871 Universal Stock Printer

Messages were typed on the keyboard and transmitted by telegraph wire. They were received in a single printed line on a one-inch paper tape. This printing telegraph was the forerunner of the teletype.

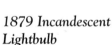

1879 Incandescent Lightbulb

Edison was not the first to experiment with electric light but he was the first to make it practical for home use. Edison also developed an entire electrical power system so that electric light could be used in homes and businesses.

1868 Vote Recorder

Edison's first patented invention that he failed to sell to Congress. It electrically recorded votes.

1847–1931

1889 Kinetograph

This early motion picture camera filmed one-minute films in the "Black Maria" studio on everything from a man sneezing to a boxing match to a ballet dancer.

1894 Kinetoscope

For 10 cents one person peered through a hole in the box to see a moving picture. The first commercial viewing was on April 14, 1896, in New York City. This one was fitted with sound tubes that were later discontinued because of technical problems.

1912 Kinetophone

A combination phonograph and kinetoscope—a complete talking picture machine. Technical problems kept this from being a commercial success. Not until the late 1920s was sound successfully combined with film—known as "talkies."

1877 Carbon Transmitter

This device amplified human voice for the telephone and microphone. Alexander Graham Bell's receiver and Edison's transmitter are the basis for today's telephone.

1893 Black Maria

The first movie studio was located at Edison's West Orange, New Jersey, laboratory. The building rotated and the roof opened so that the stage was always facing the sun. He filmed one-minute movies on various subjects that later could be viewed on Kinetoscopes.

1875 Etheroscope

In this black box Edison discovered strange sparks he called etheric force. He actually had discovered the principle of sound waves, which would be used to invent the radio years later.

AUTHOR'S NOTE

Thomas Edison contributed more to the twentieth century than any other inventor. It wasn't easy though—he failed many times before he succeeded. His trial-and-error method was the same for each invention. How does this work? What if I did this? "Genius is 1 percent inspiration and 99 percent perspiration," he once said.

At his Menlo Park and West Orange laboratories, Edison had many people working for him—all skilled craftsmen: carpenters, glassblowers, machinists, electricians, mathematicians, draftsmen, clock makers, and more. It was a team effort, and each member of the team provided a different expertise. Edison would sketch his idea on a piece of paper and then an assistant would begin work on creating it. Edison worked alongside each of them until they found a solution. Often they worked late into the night.

To see Thomas Edison's inventions I visited the Edison National Historic Site in West Orange, New Jersey. I wanted to see firsthand just what his inventions looked like and how they worked. I even watched a movie of a boxing match on a *Kinetoscope*. Later I traveled to Milan, Ohio, to see the home where he was born. I stepped back in time at Greenfield Village in Dearborn, Michigan; the village houses Edison's Menlo Park laboratory. There I listened to the actual recording of "Mary Had a Little Lamb" on his *tinfoil phonograph*. Finally, I visited the Port Huron train depot where Edison worked as a boy, selling newspapers.

Through hard work, curiosity, and imagination, Thomas Edison changed the way we live and work. Whenever you talk on a telephone, switch on a lamp, listen to the radio, play music, or go to the movies, you are a beneficiary of Thomas Edison's genius. And it all started when he was just a boy. Can you think of an invention that would improve your life?

SELECTED BIBLIOGRAPHY

Edison National Historic Site. *Edison*. West Orange, N.J.: National Parks Service US Department of the Interior, 1998.

Pretzer, William S., ed. *Working at Inventing: Thomas A. Edison and the Menlo Park Experience.* Baltimore: The Johns Hopkins University Press, 2002. First published 1989 by Henry Ford Museum & Greenfield Village.

Thomas Edison and His Menlo Park Laboratory. Dearborn, Mich.: Henry Ford Museum & Greenfield Village, n.d.

SUGGESTED WEBSITES

Edison & Ford Winter Estates: www.edison-ford-estate.com

Edison Birthplace Museum: www.tomedison.org

Edison National Historic Site: www.nps.gov/edis

The Henry Ford Museum & Greenfield Village: www.hfmgv.org/exhibits/Edison/default.asp

The Thomas Edison Depot Museum: www.phmuseum.org/depot/depot.htm

Thomas Alva Edison Memorial Tower and Menlo Park Museum:
www.edisonnj.org/menlopark/museum.asp